Welcome to Inky Chris

Volume 10 in the series

A wonderland of 32 magically-enchanting, festive illustrations, await your imagination!

From summer Christmas scenes, pets climbing presents, whimsical elves on shelves… to the chocolate factory, penguin ice bar, and Santa's chaotic mail room… there is plenty to captivate and entertain.

I always suggest (and do myself) placing a blank sheet under your work page to protect the illustration beneath from bleed-through of certain pens.

To view pages I have coloured from my books, inspiration, and forthcoming book details, please visit my Helenclaireart Facebook page (where I post my colouring tutorial videos!) or my website: www.Helenclaireart.co.uk

The series so far:
Inky Ocean, Inky Garden, Inky Mandalas, Inky Mandalas Mix, Inky Extreme, Inky Dinky Blossom, Inky Lifestyle, Inky Galaxy, Inky Whimsy… and now Inky Christmas!

I hope my designs bring you many hours of enjoyment.

Helen xx

Copyright © 2015 Helen Elliston
All rights reserved.
ISBN: 1537720759
ISBN-13: 978-1537720753

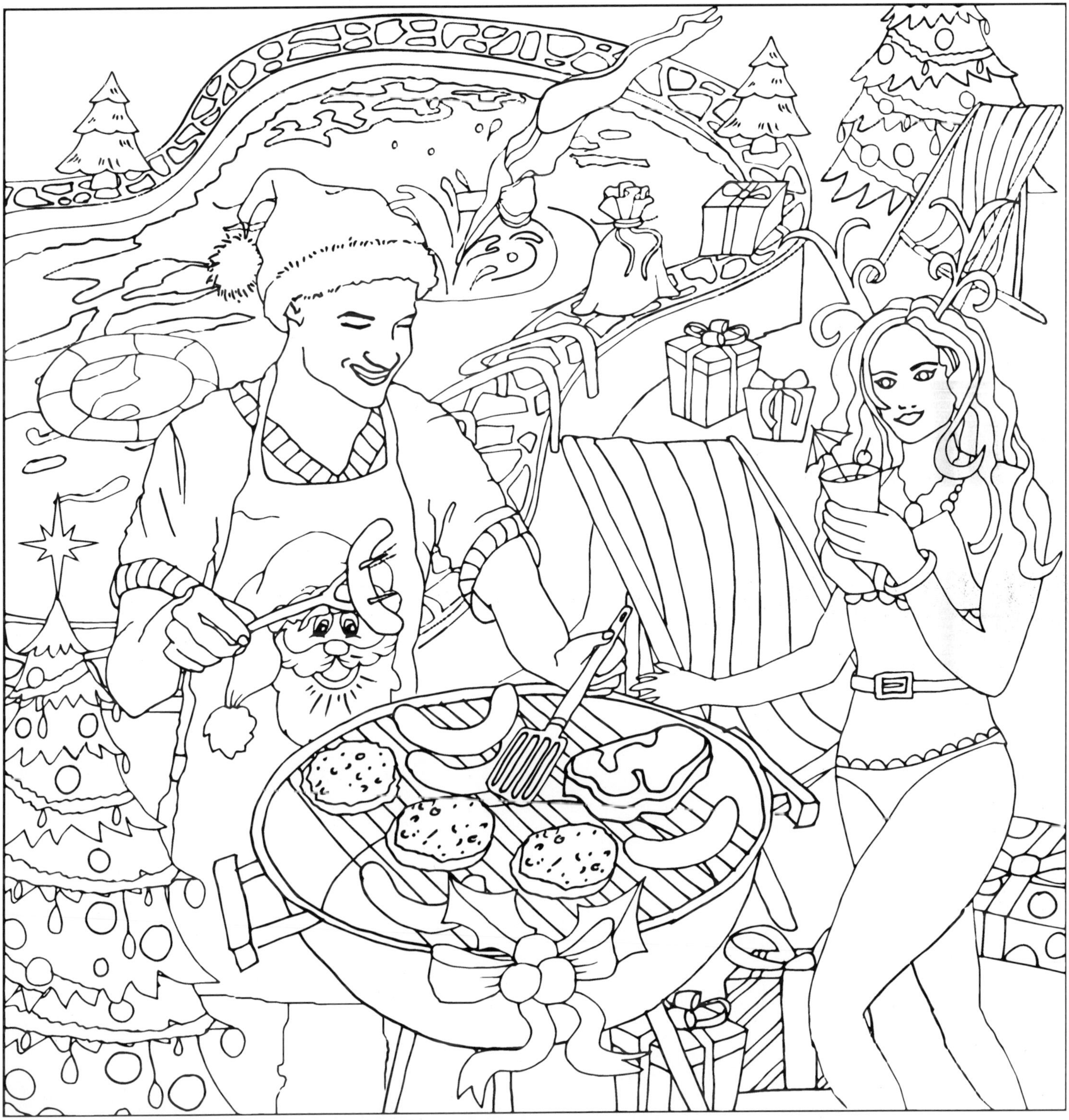

Ho Ho Ho!
Seasons Greetings
NORTH POLE
AIR MAIL
EXPRESS
With Love

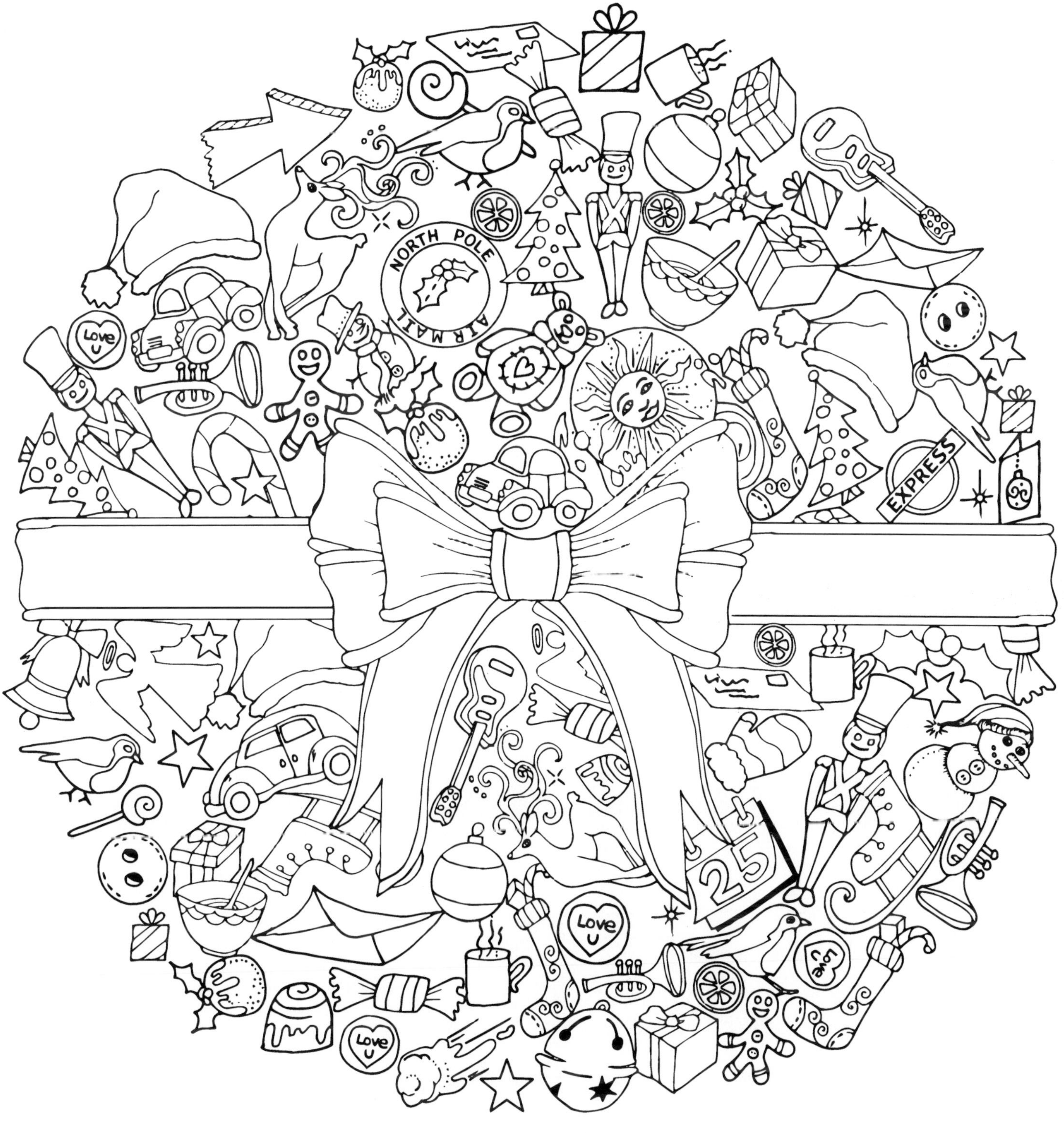
NORTH POLE
AIR MAIL
Love U
EXPRESS
25
Love U
Love U
Love U

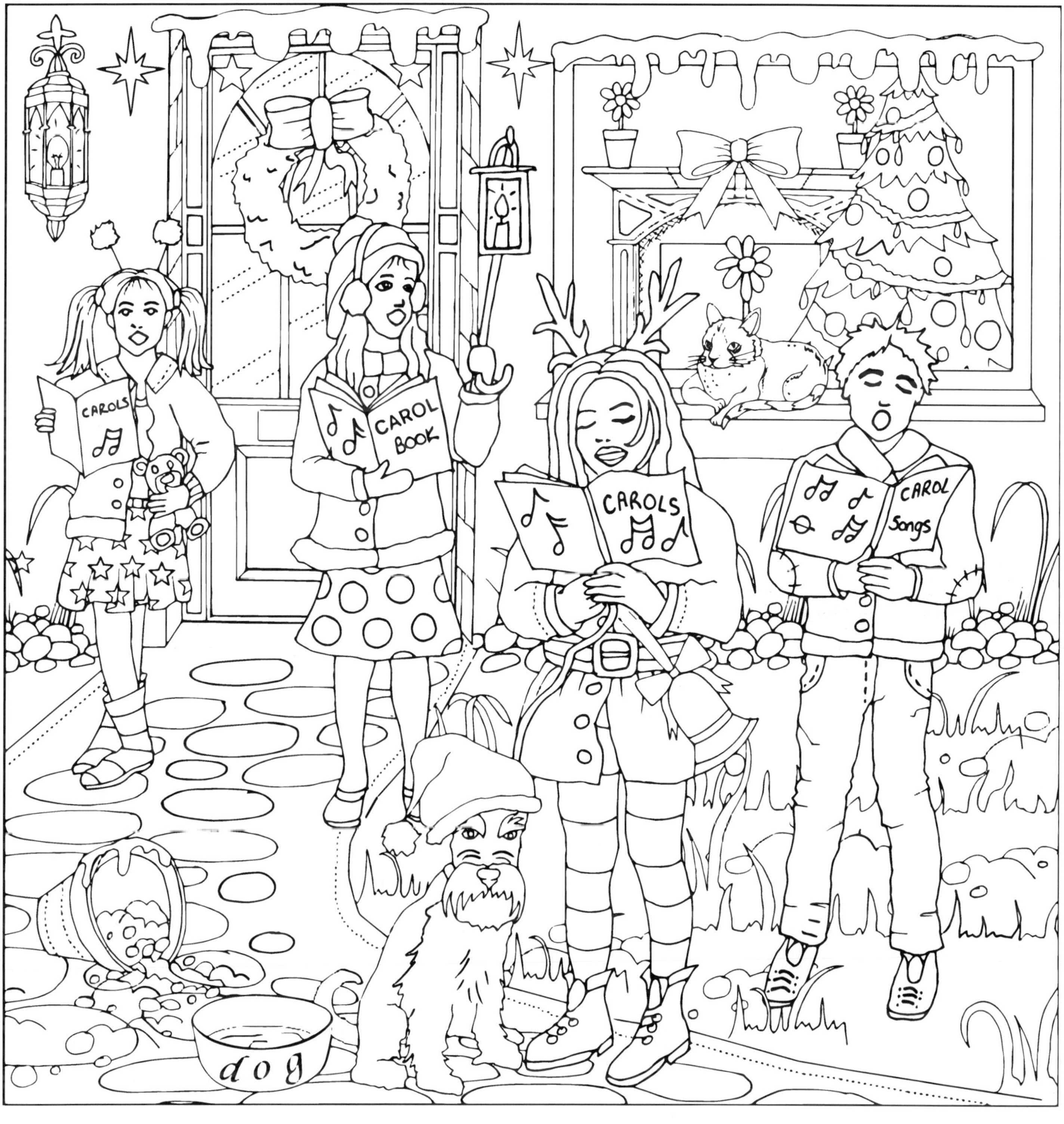
CAROLS
CAROL BOOK
CAROLS
CAROL Songs
dog

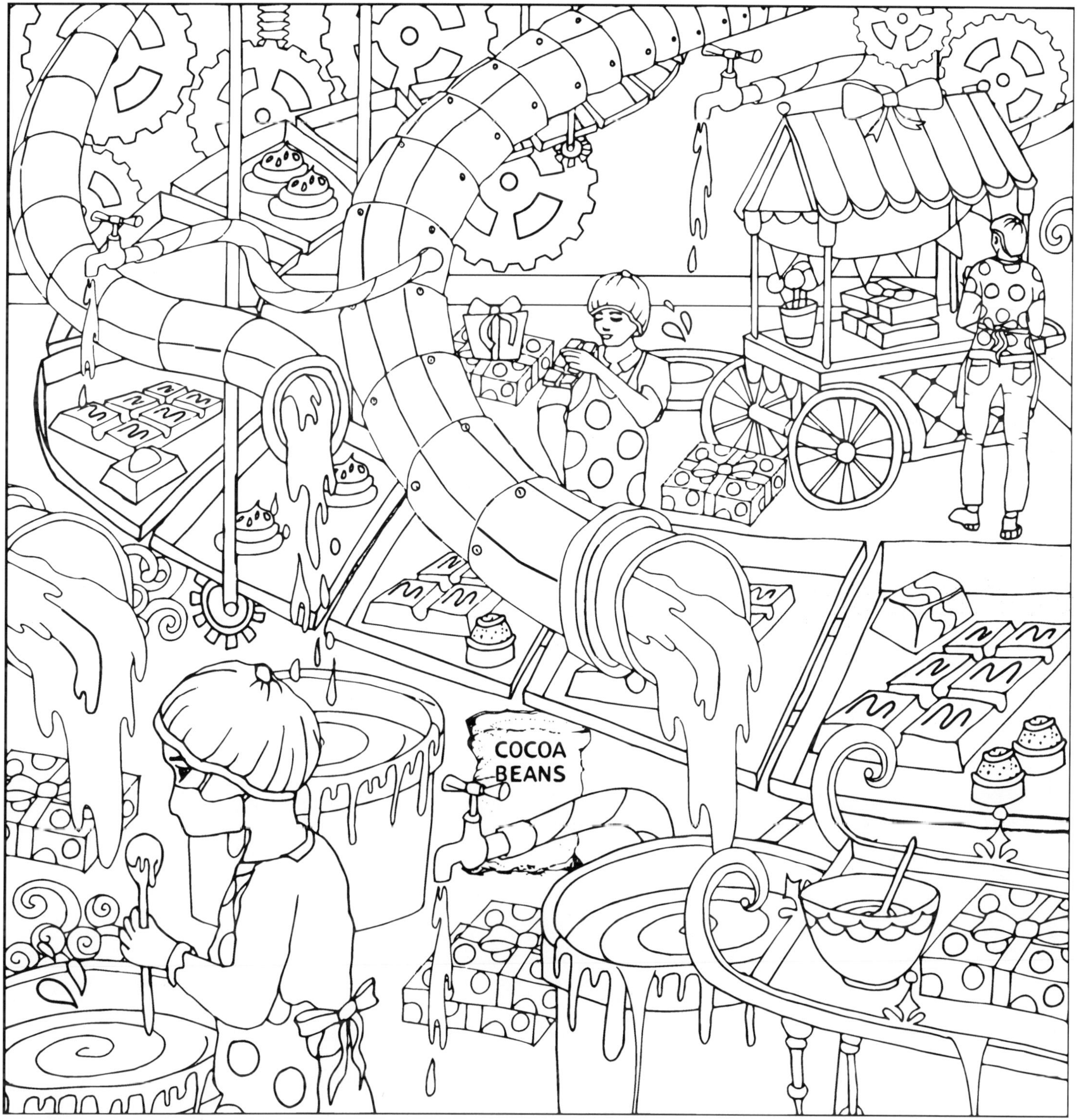
COCOA
BEANS

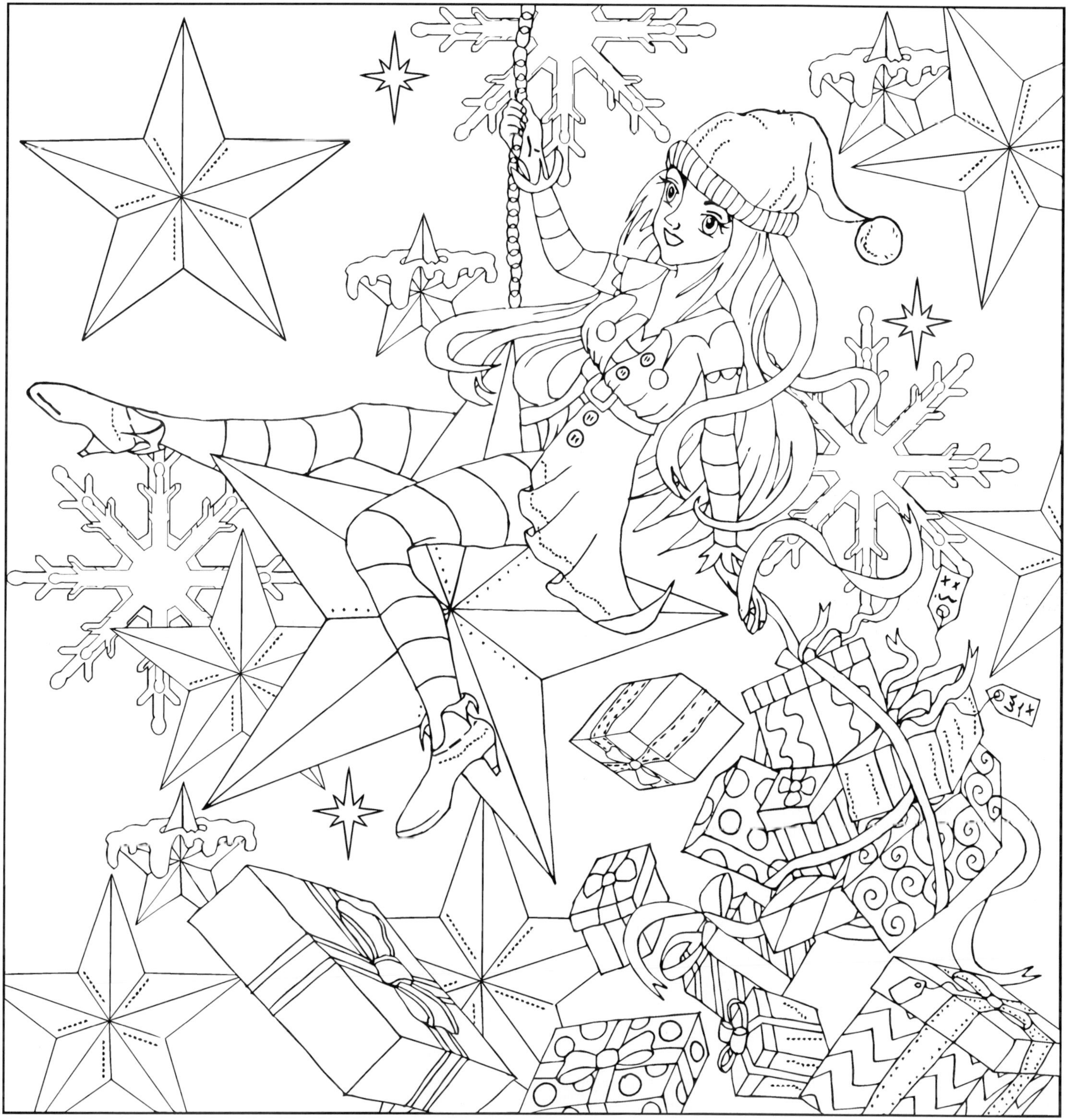

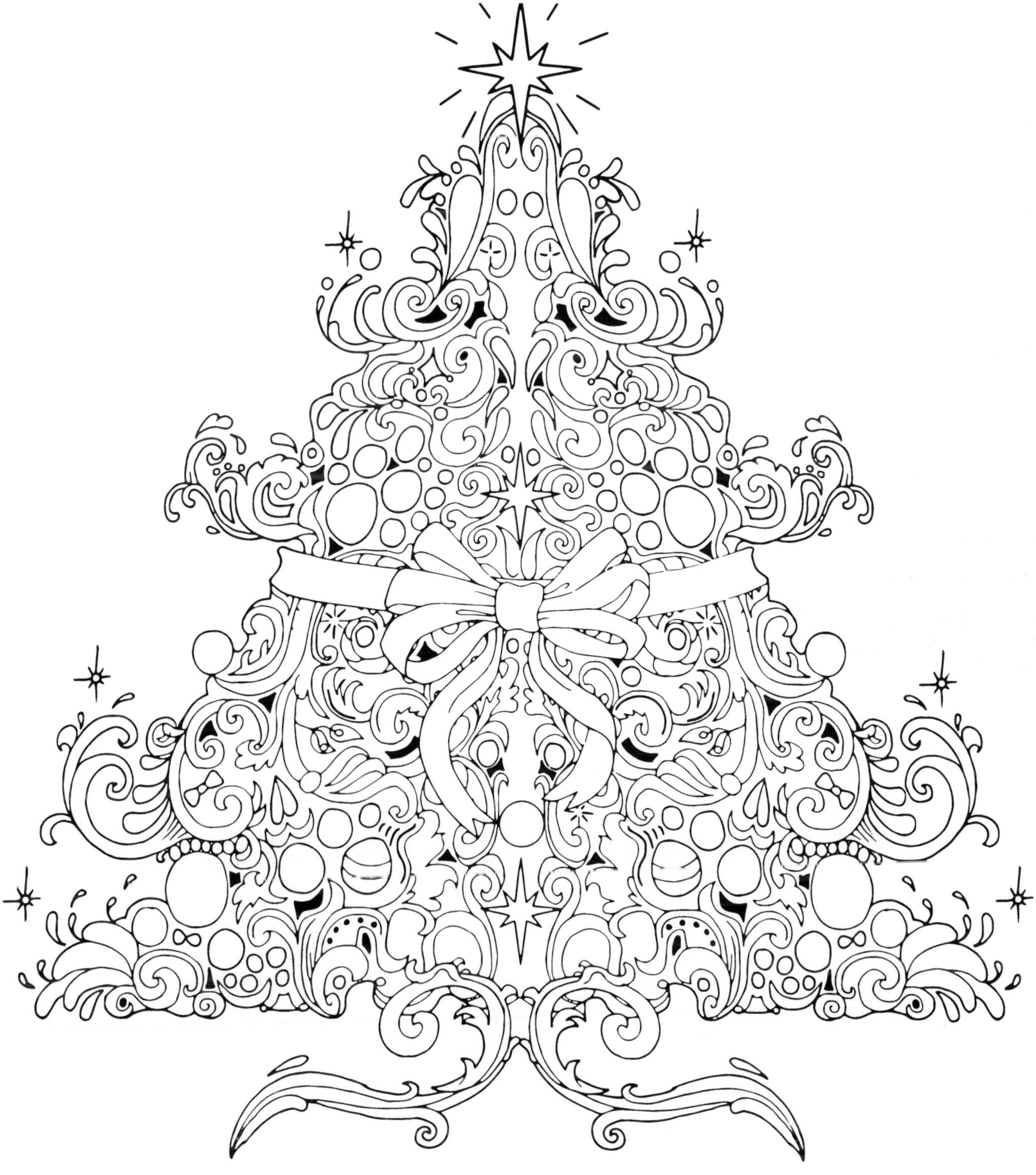

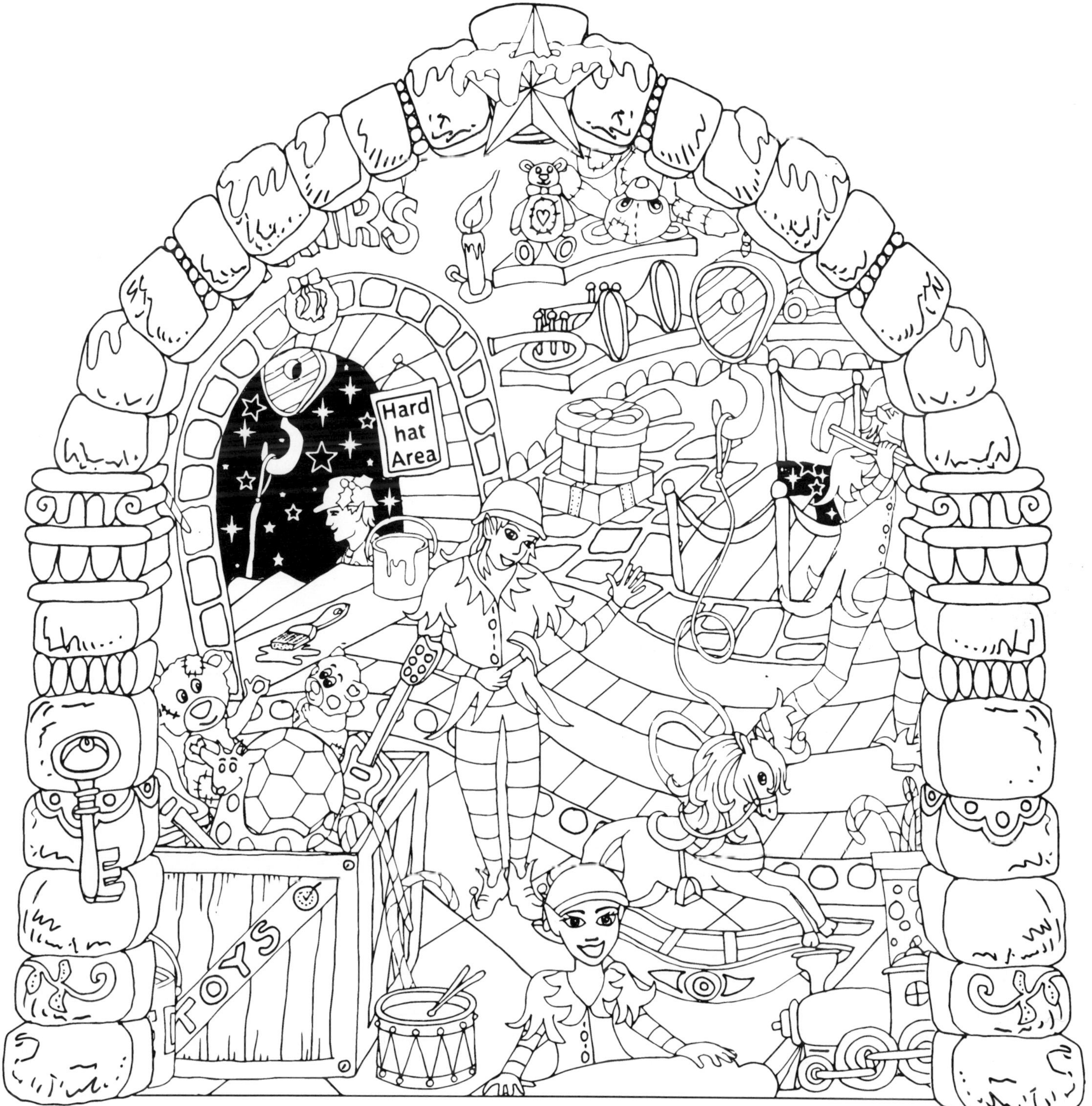
Hard
hat
Area
TOYS

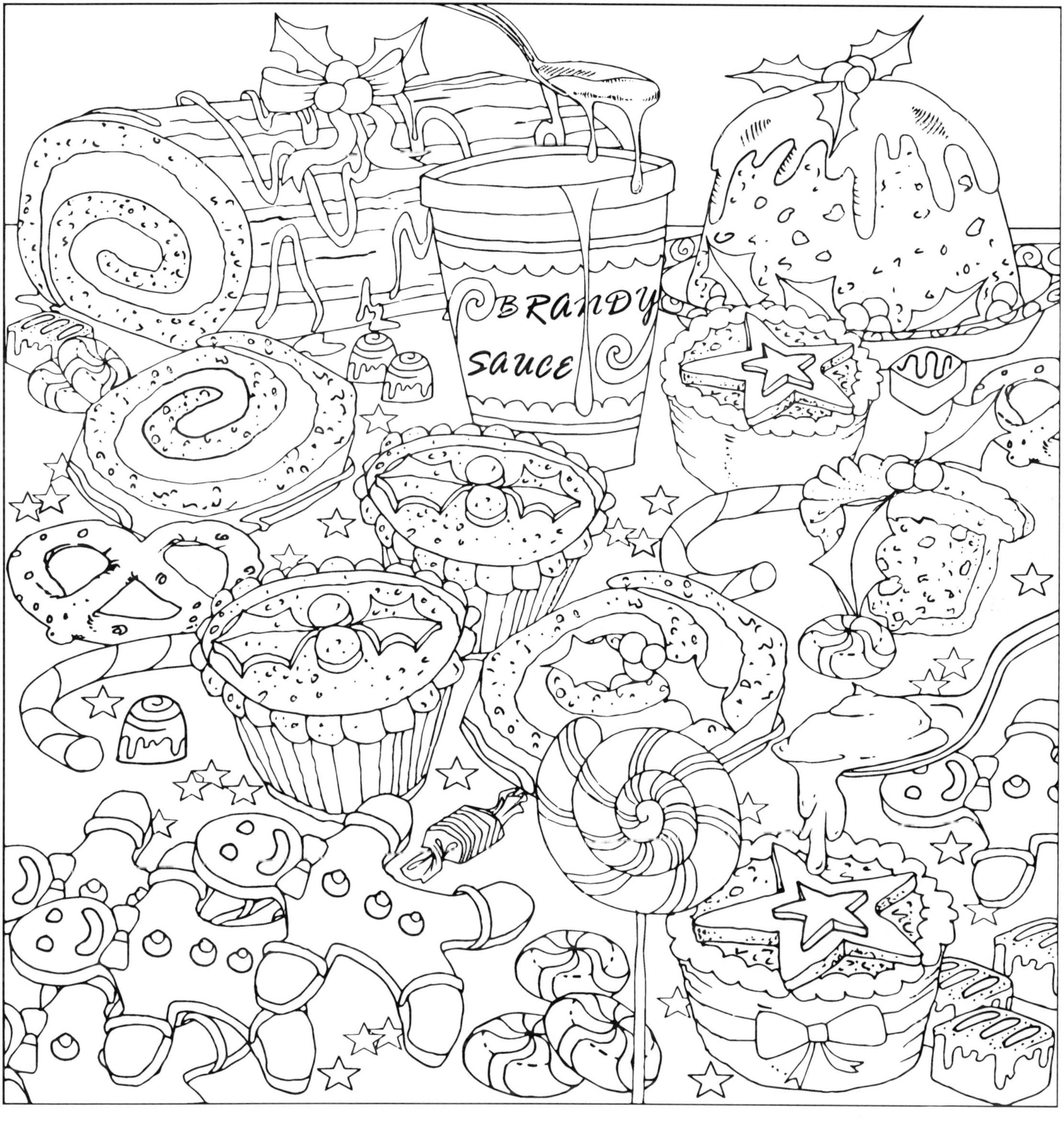
BRANDY
SAUCE

SNOWFALL
TIDINGS
WEATHER
SEASONS
XMAS
NORTH POLE
HOLIDAYS
WISHES
MAPS

MERRY CHRISTMAS

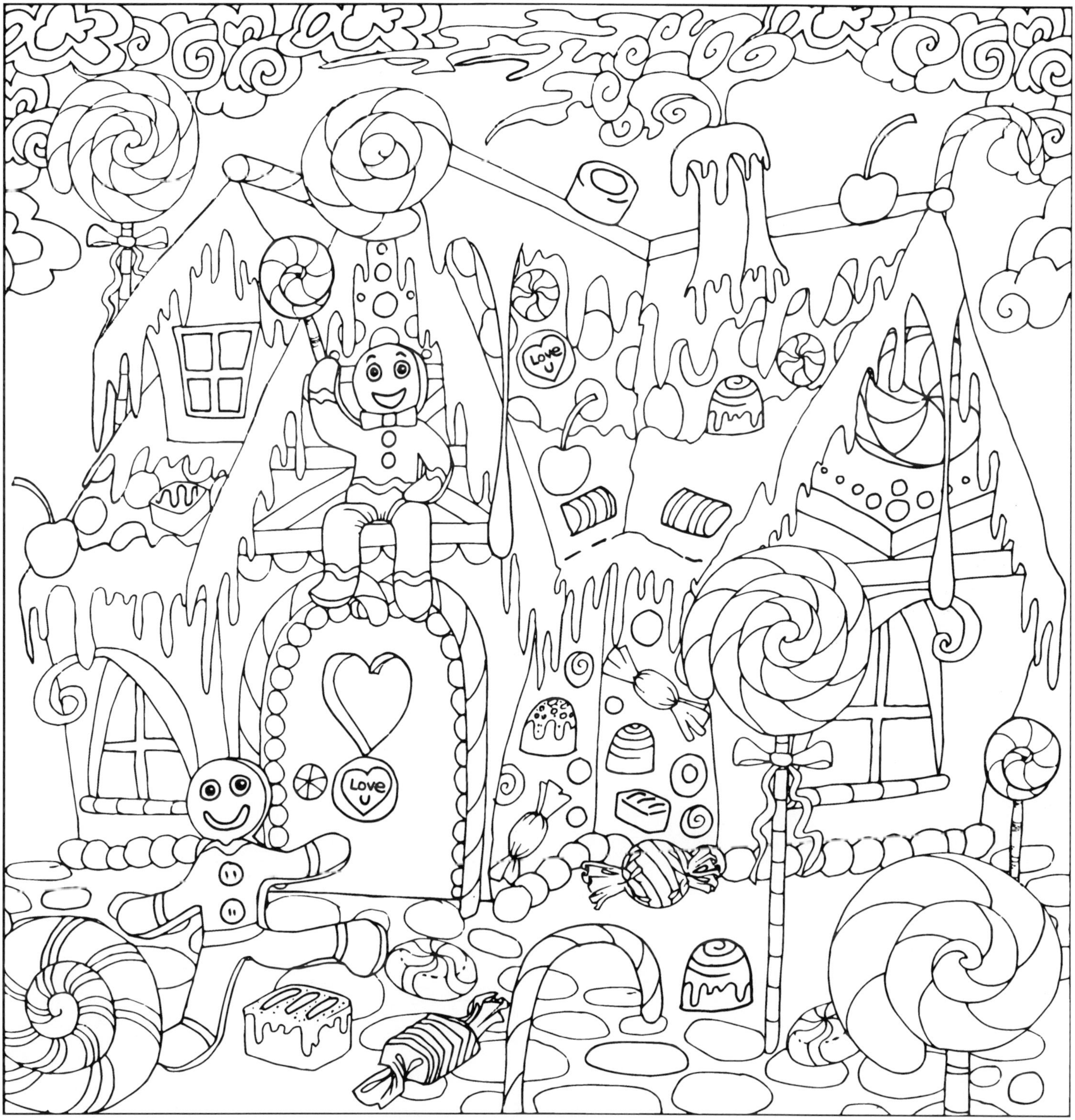
Love U
Love U

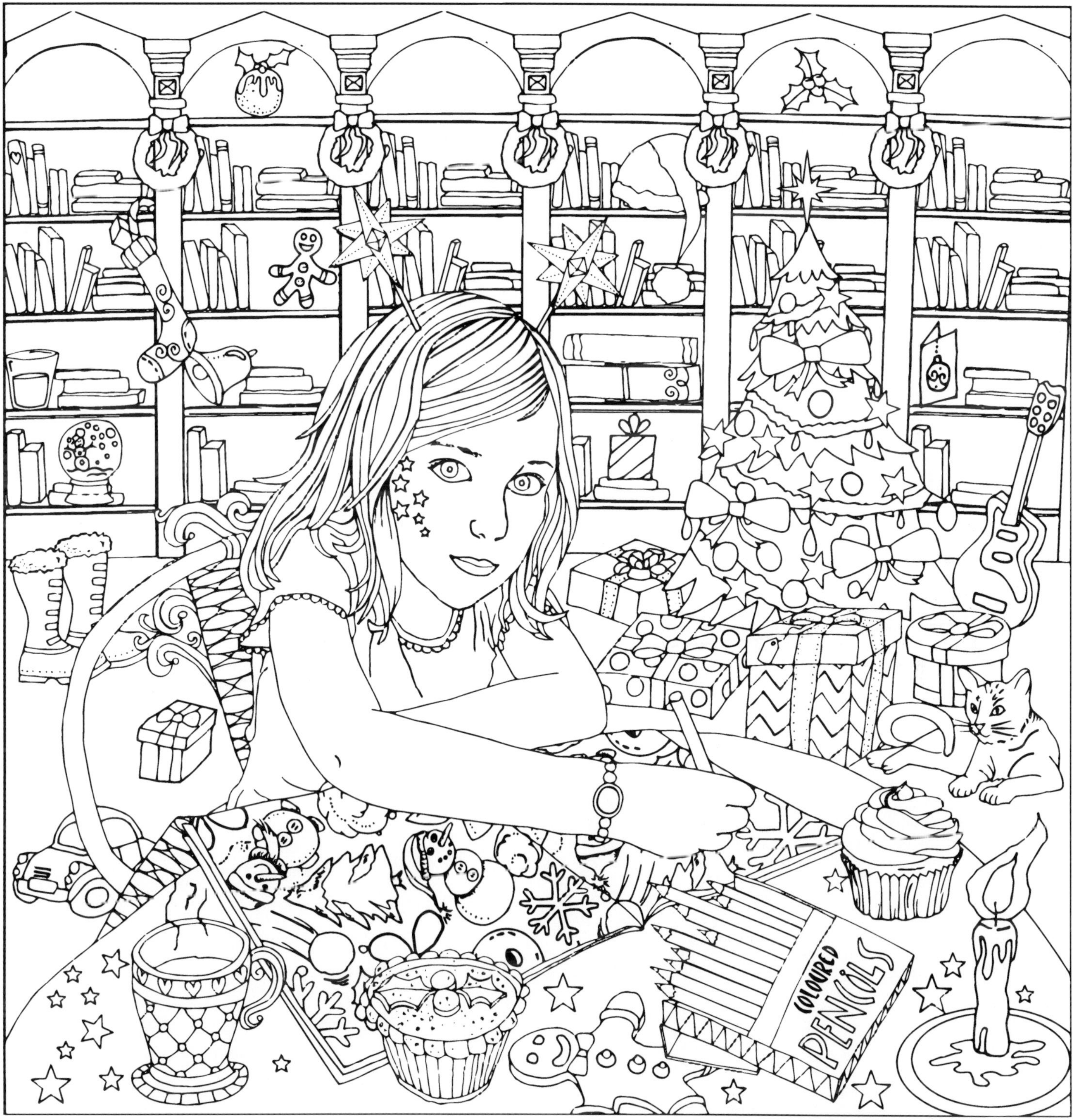
COLOURED
PENCILS

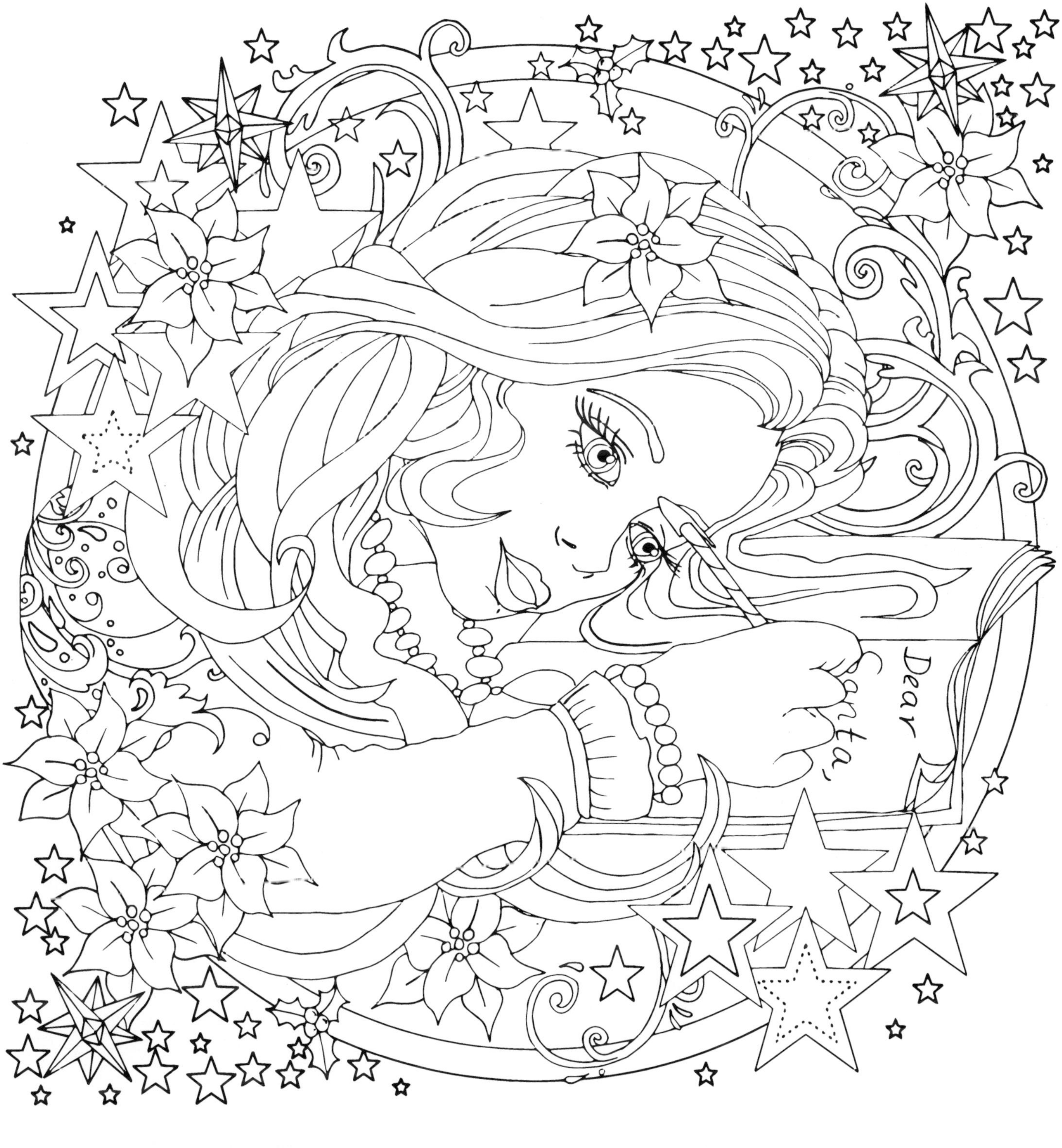
Dear

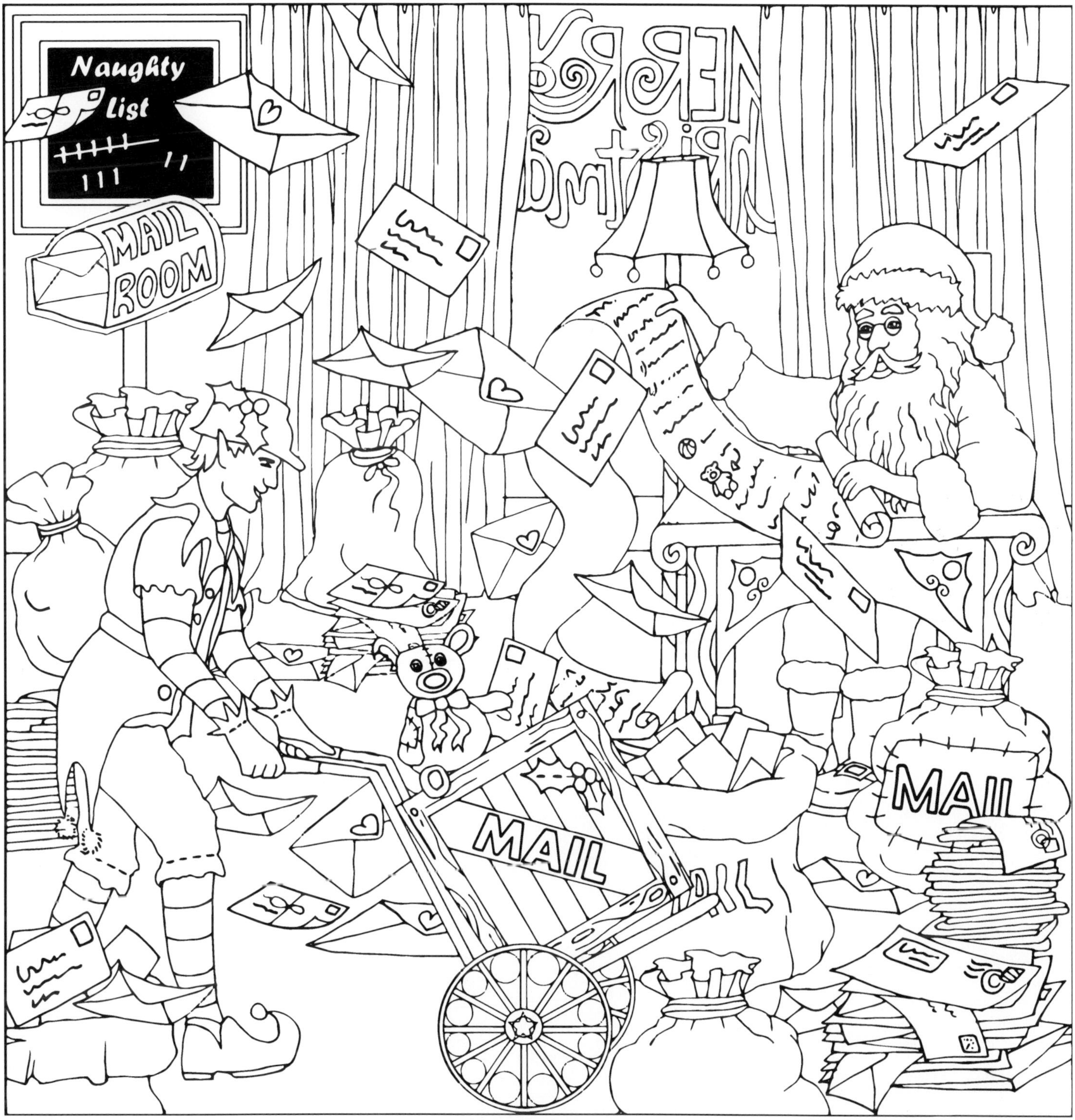
Naughty List
MAIL ROOM
MAIL
MAIL

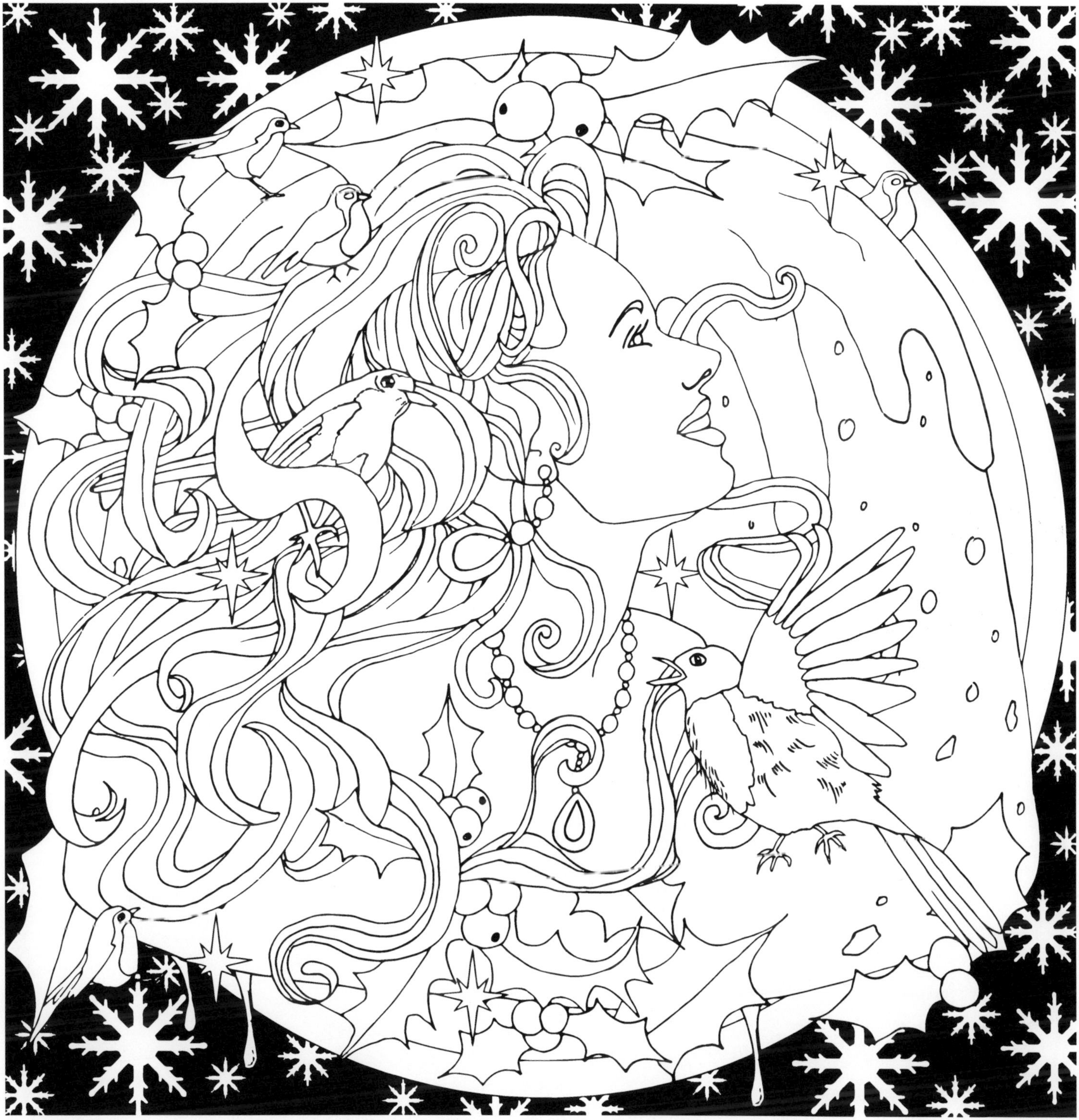

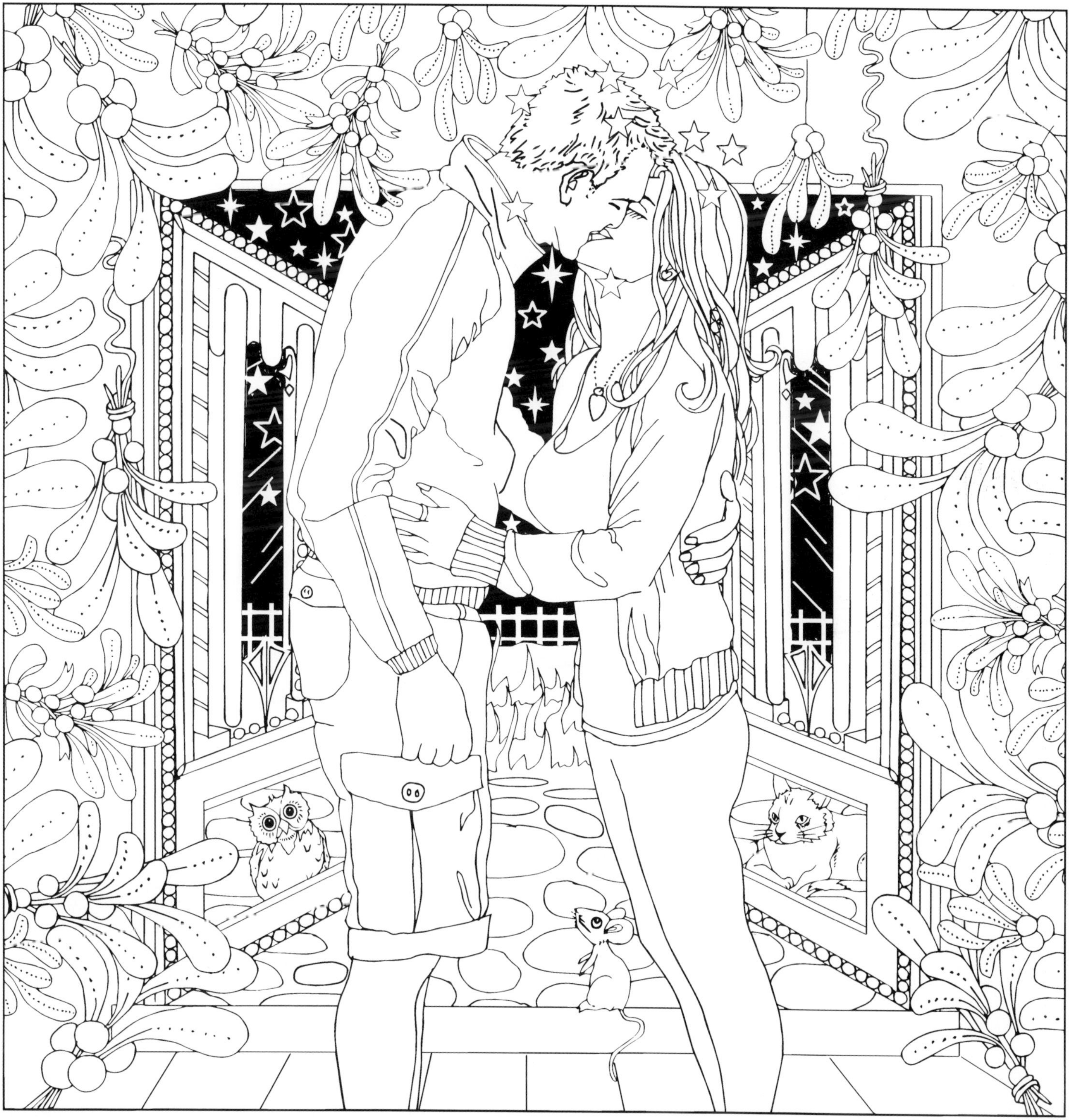

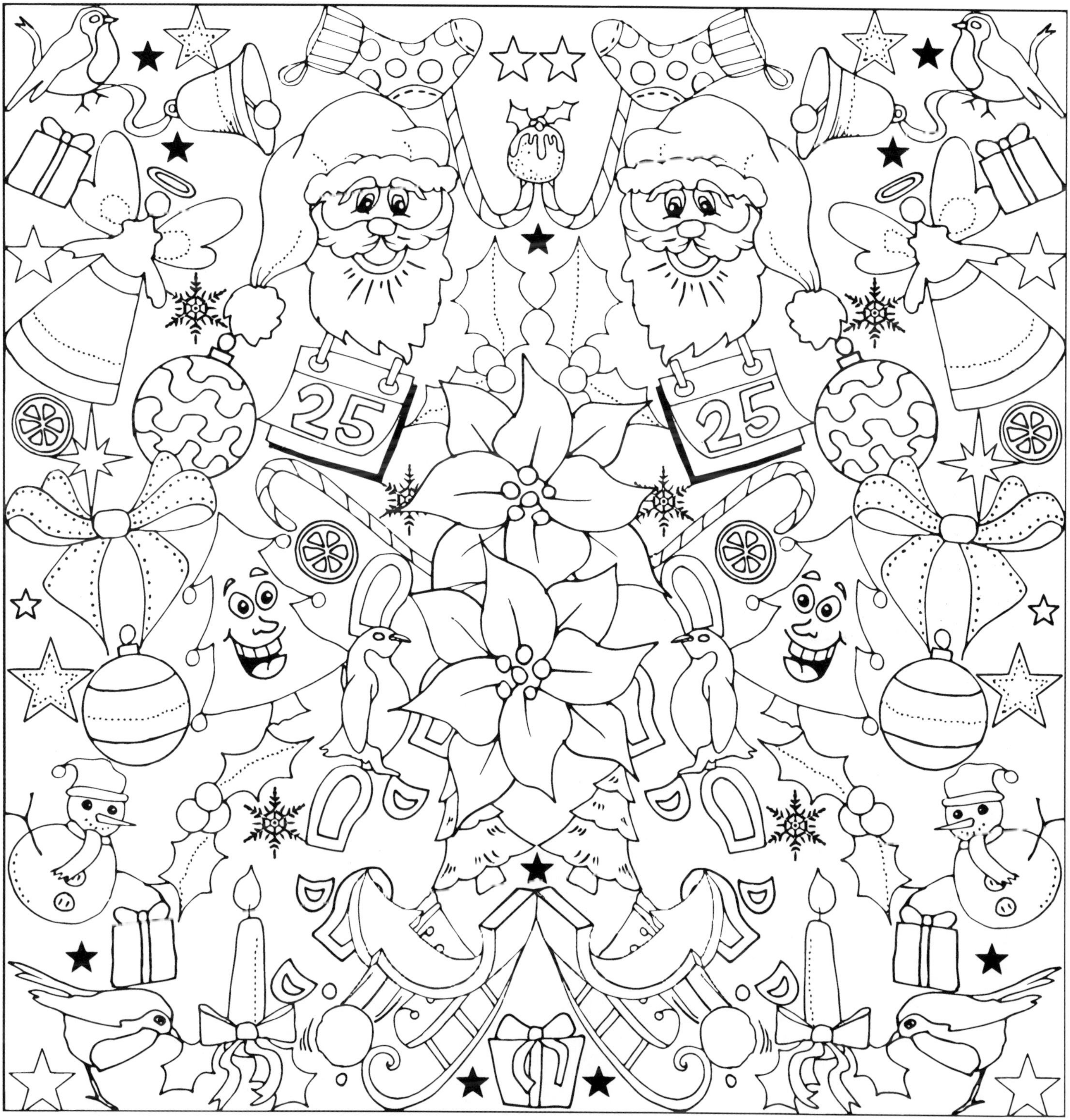
25
25

WELCOME
TO THE
NORTH POLE
RUNWAY
ELF WORKSHOP
TURN RIGHT
MAIL ROOM
Santa's
CHOCOLATE
Factory
Deliveries
CAFE
STABLES
Grotto

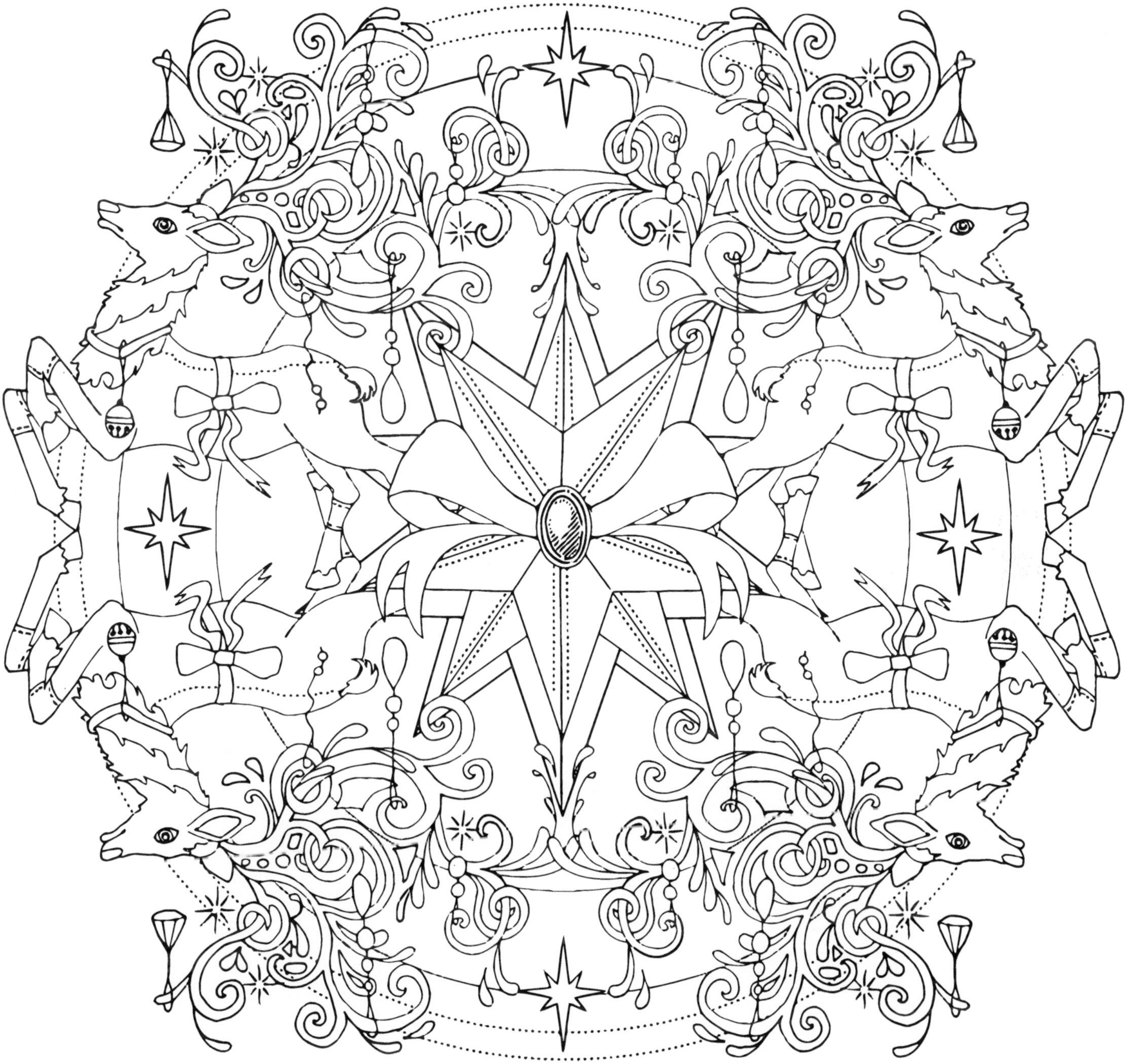

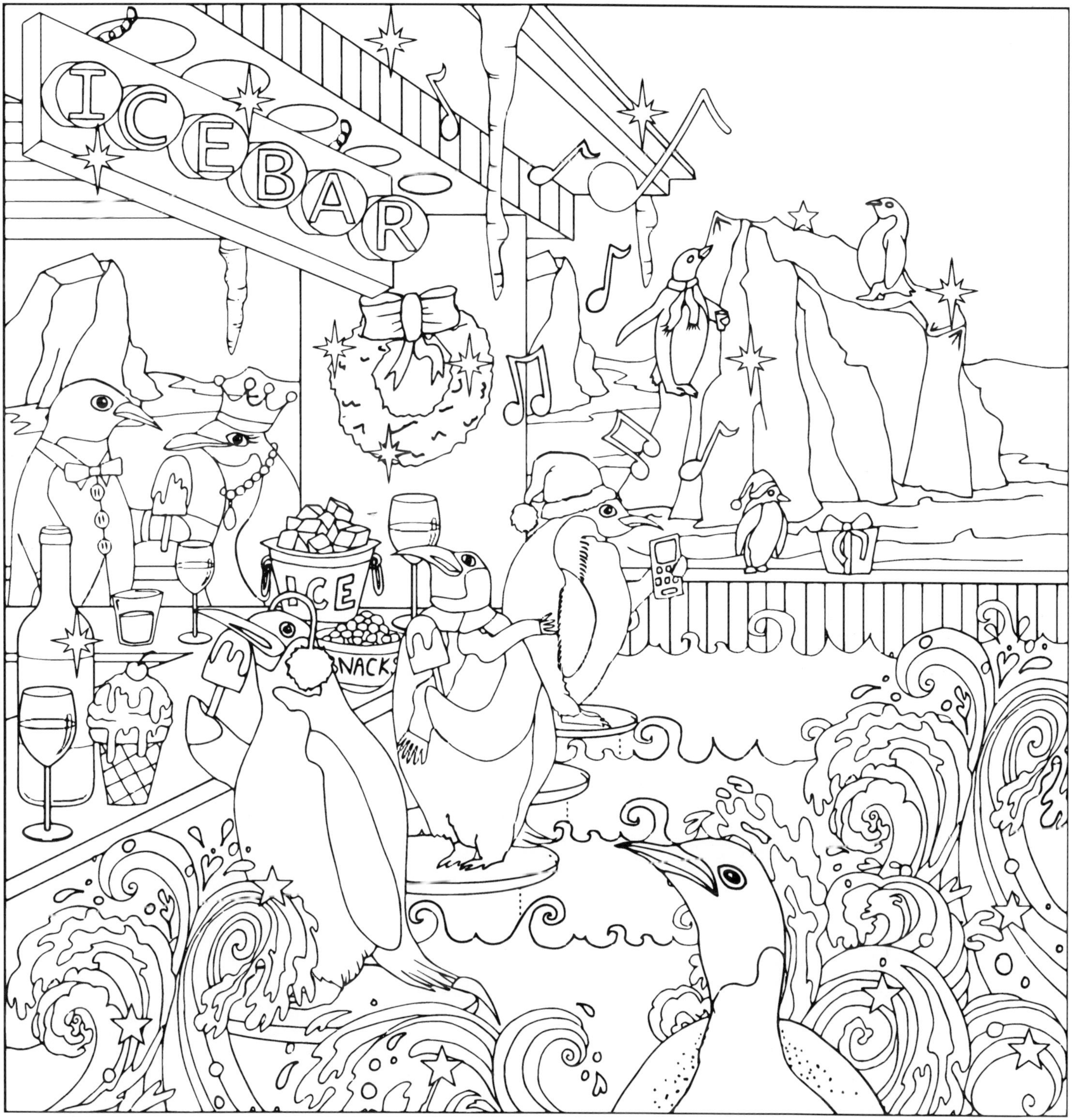
ICE BAR
ICE
SNACKS

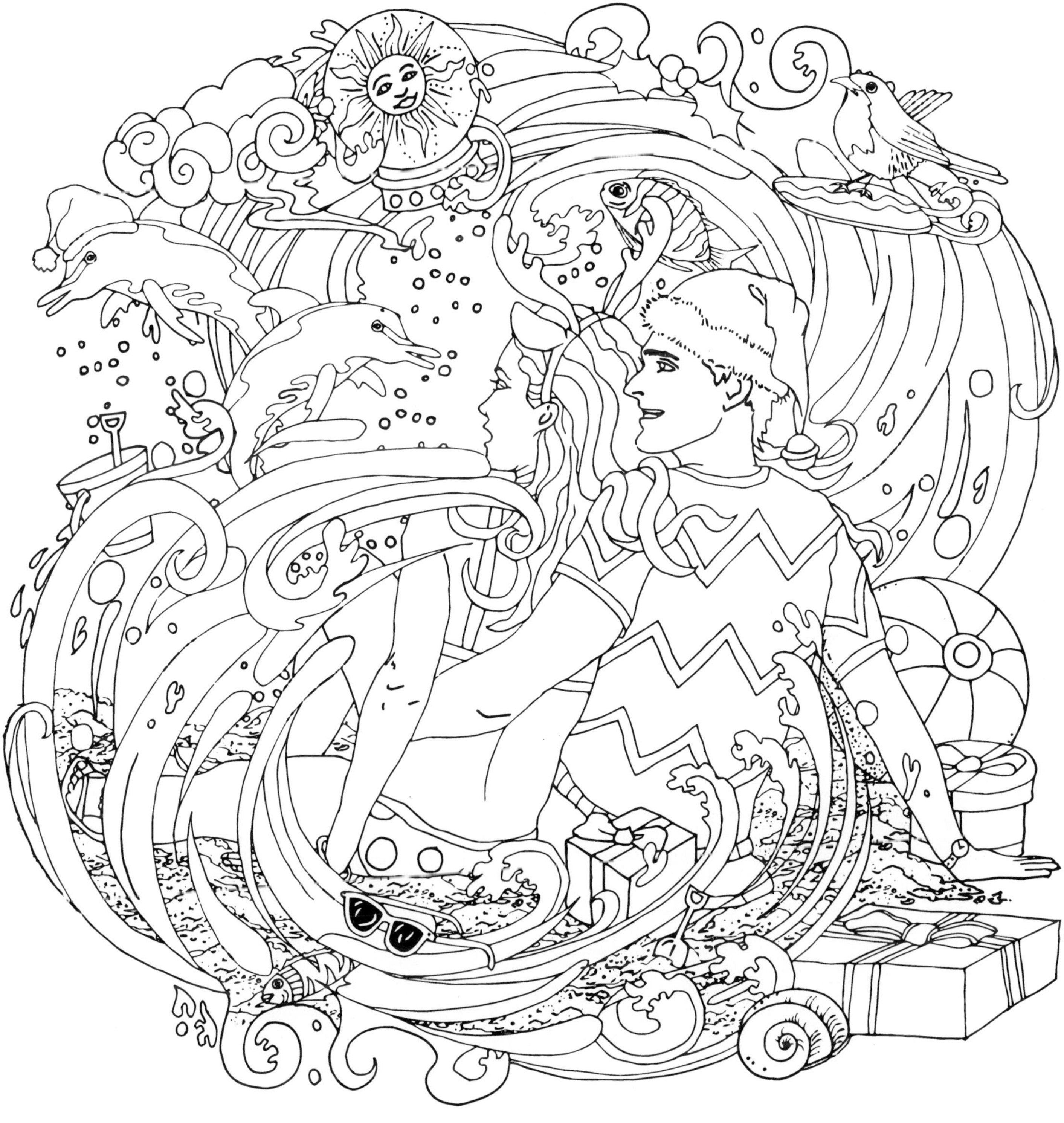

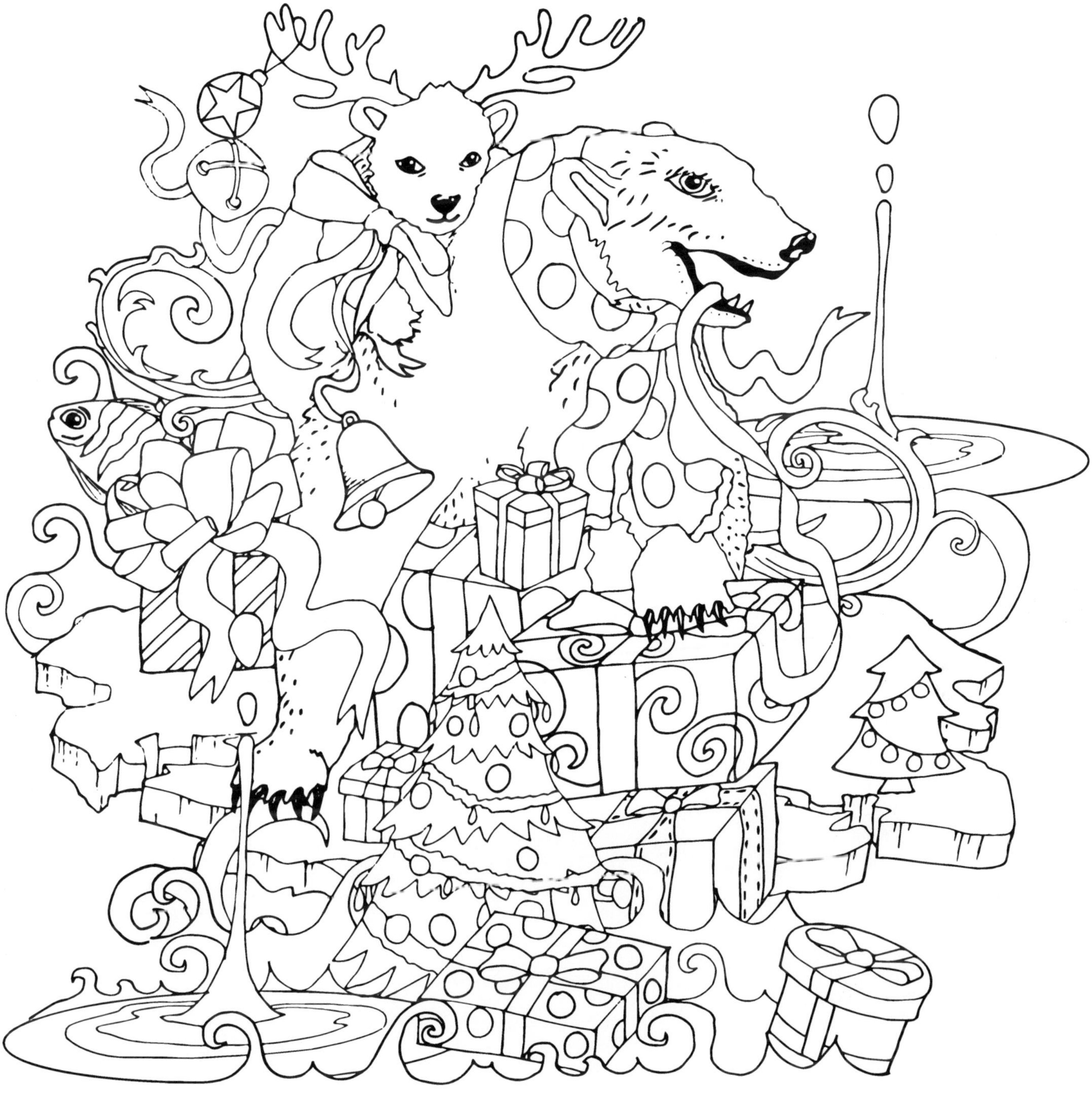

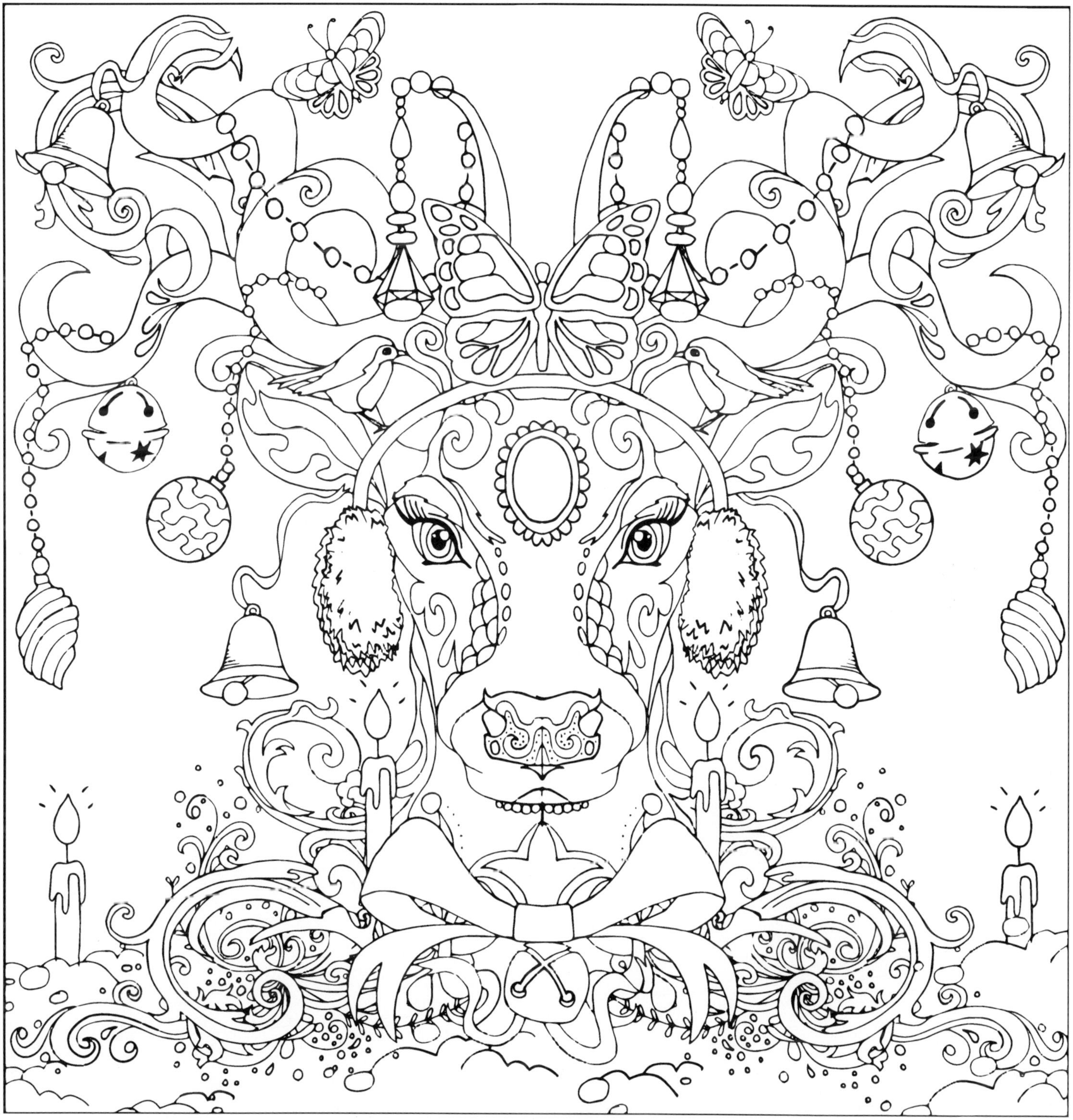

Official Letter

Dear Santa Claus,

My name is:

I have been GOOD ☐ NAUGHTY ☐ this year.

I would really like some of these gifts / wishes please:

Many thanks
x

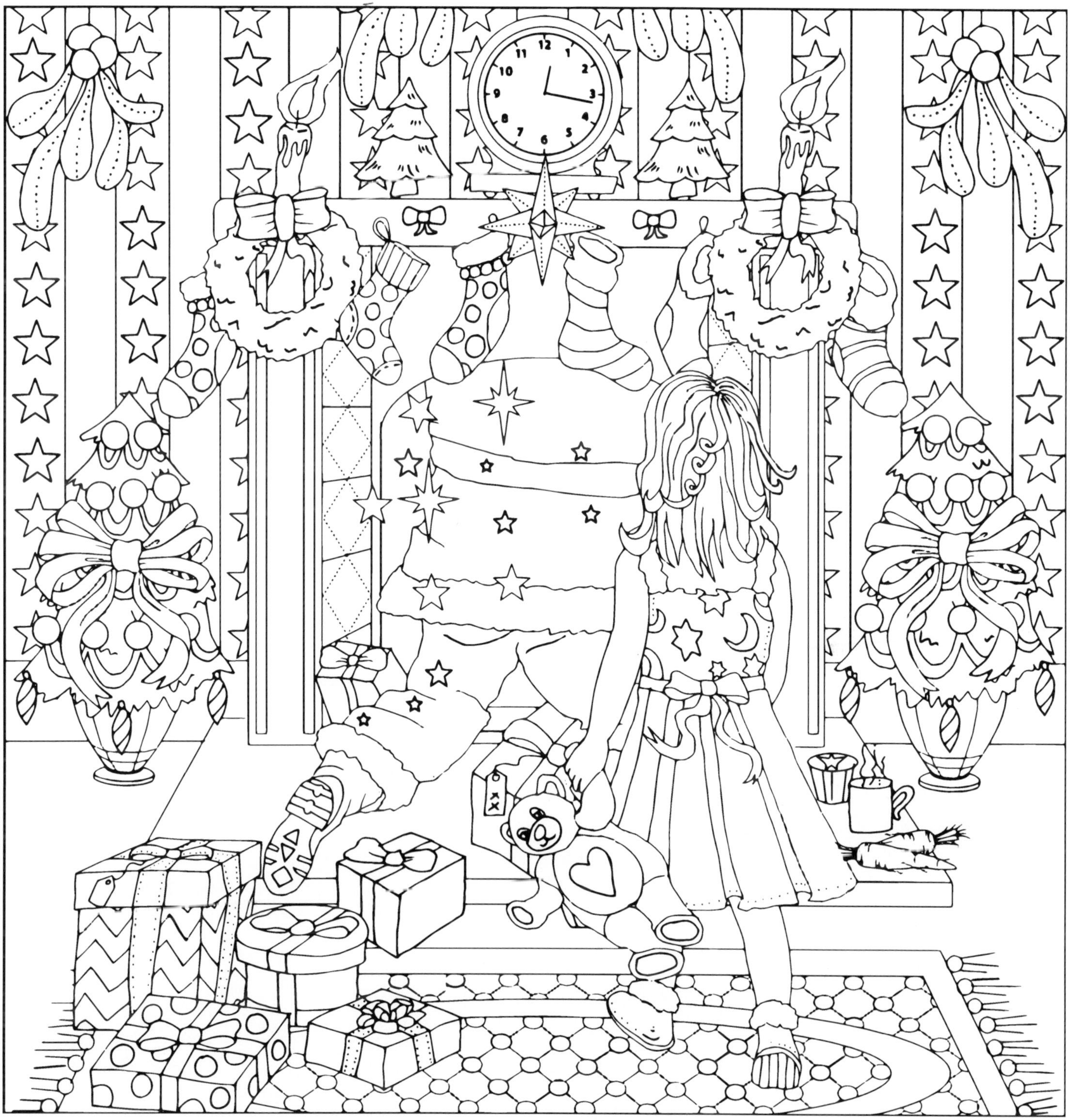
12
1
2
3
4
5
6
7
8
9
10
11
XX

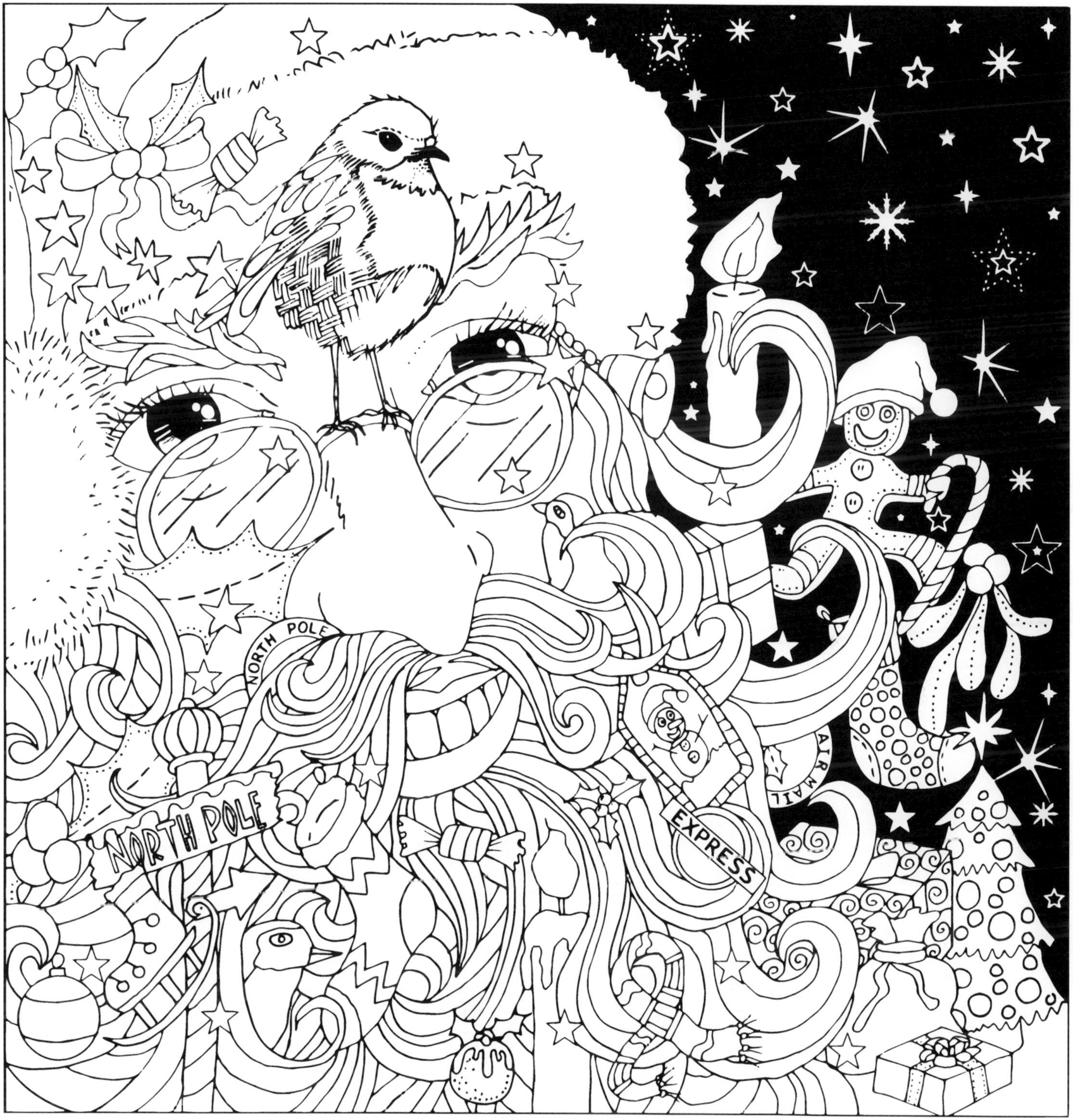
NORTH POLE
NORTH POLE
AIR MAIL
EXPRESS

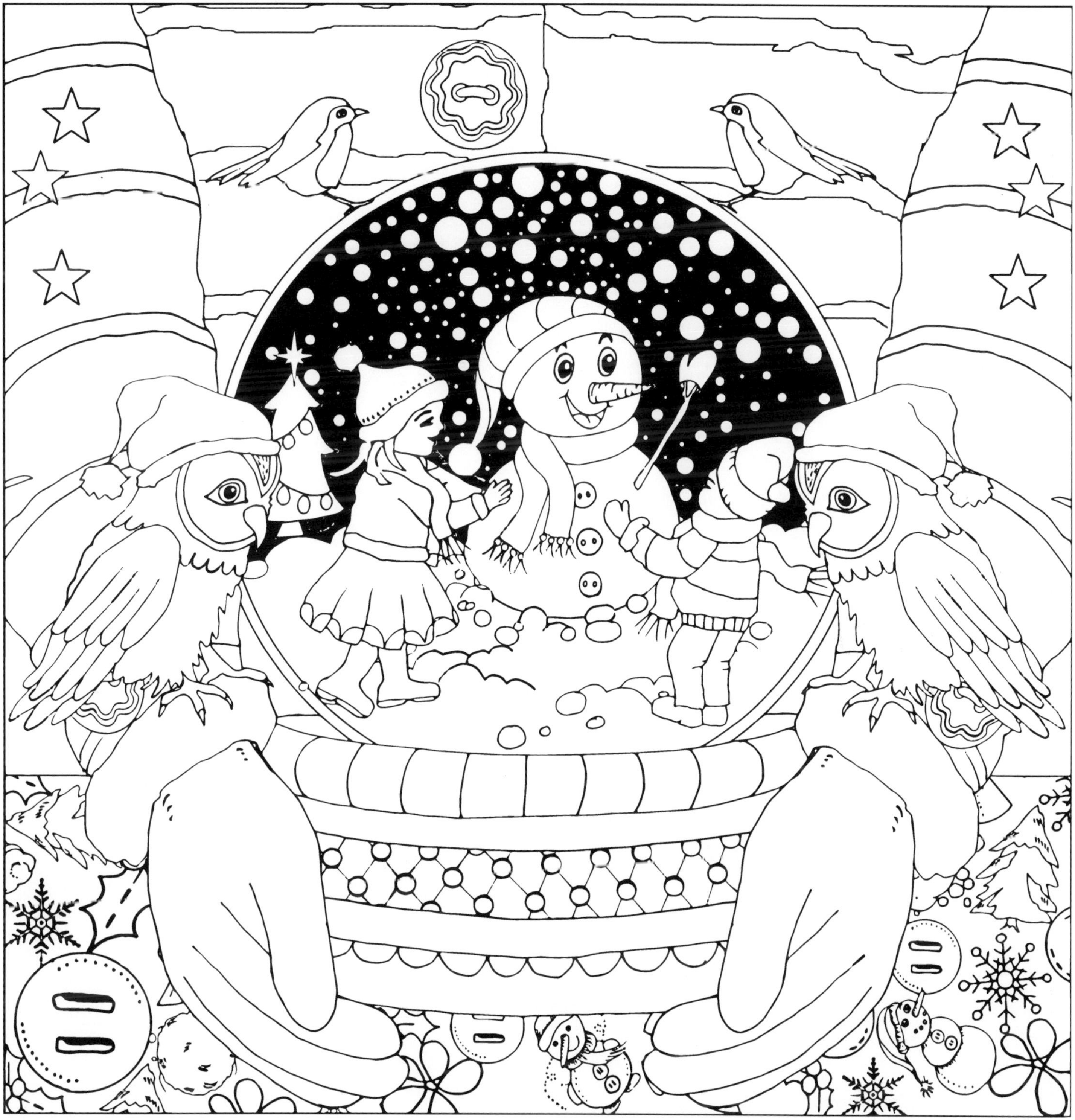

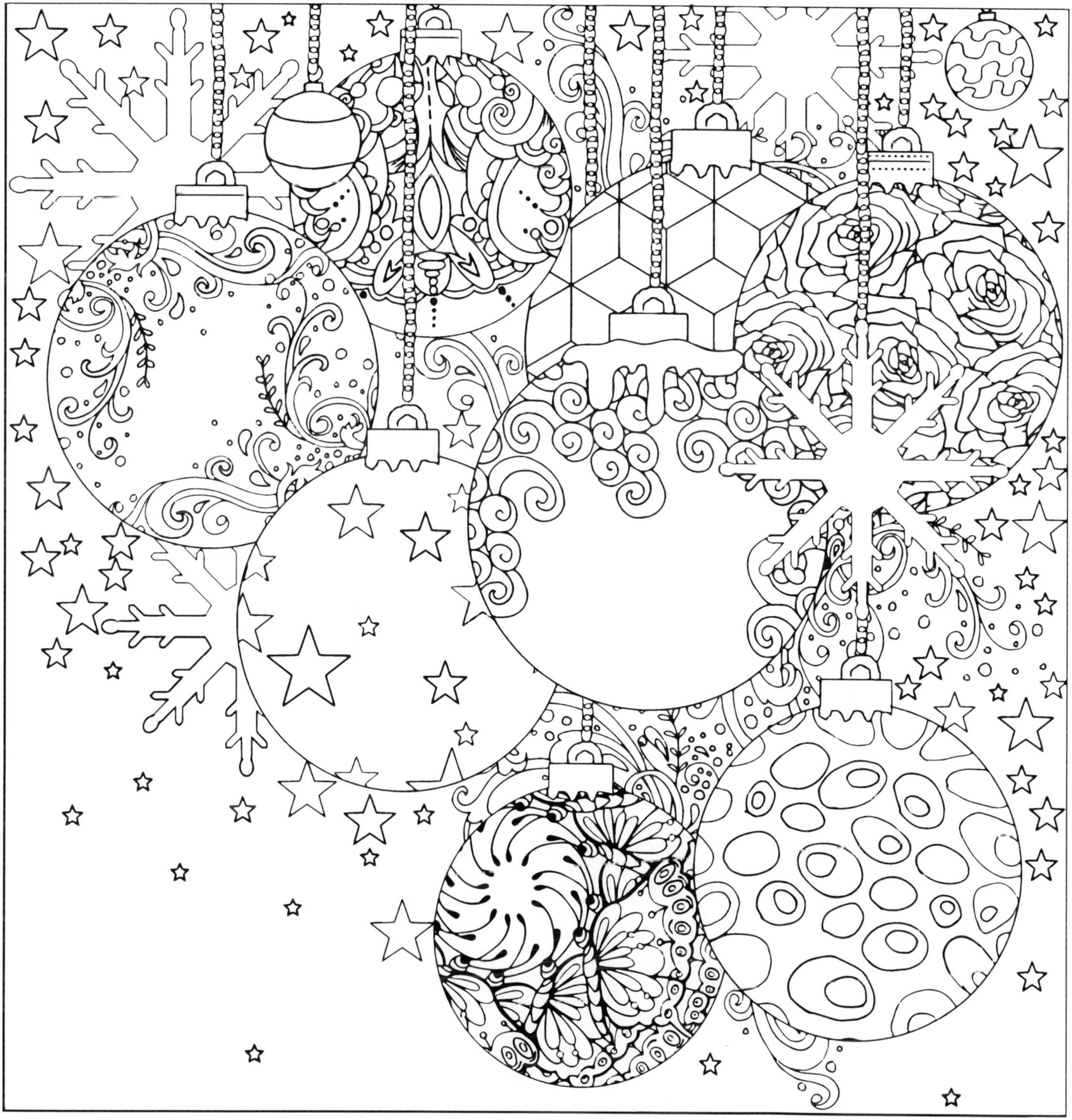

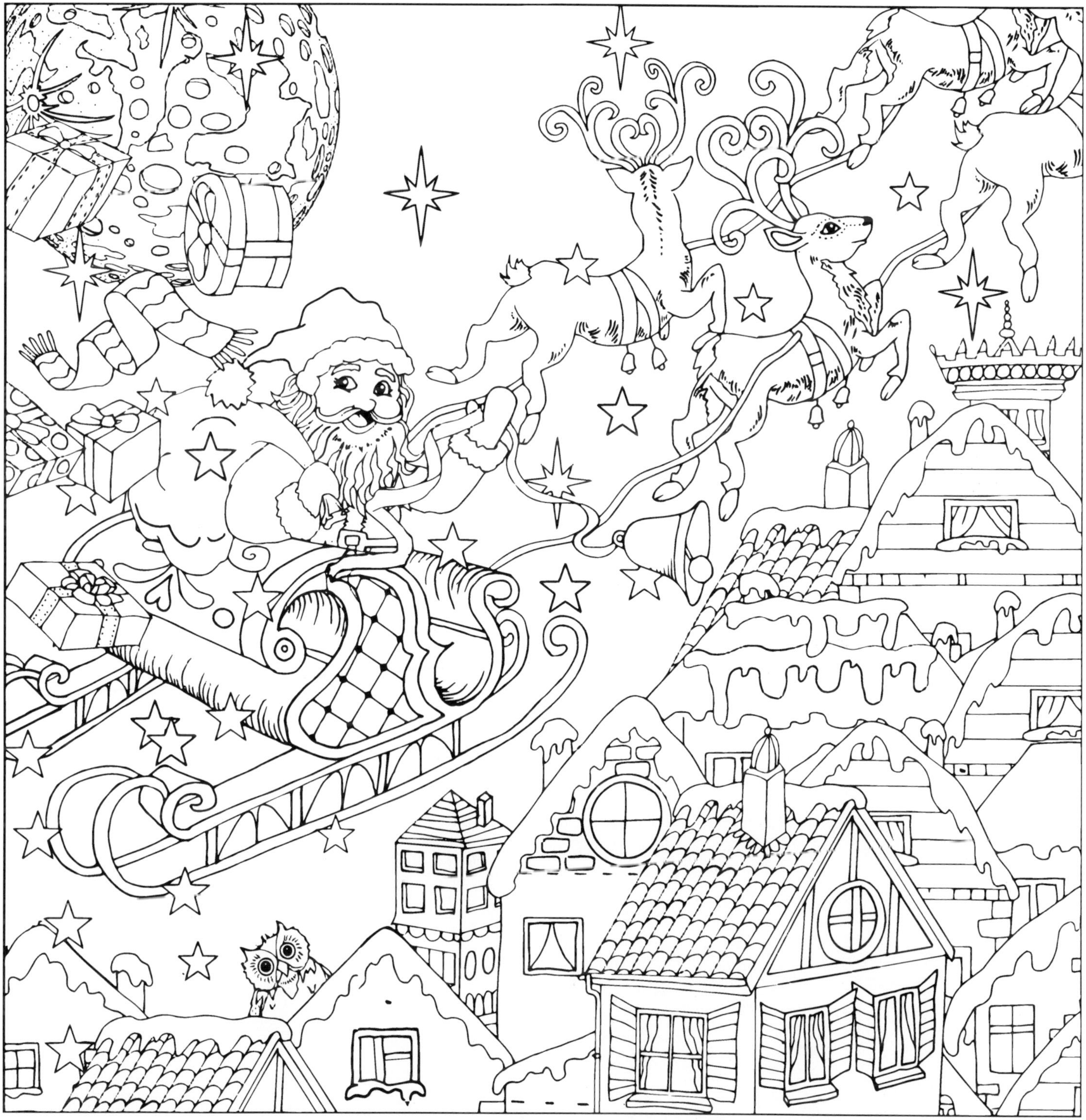

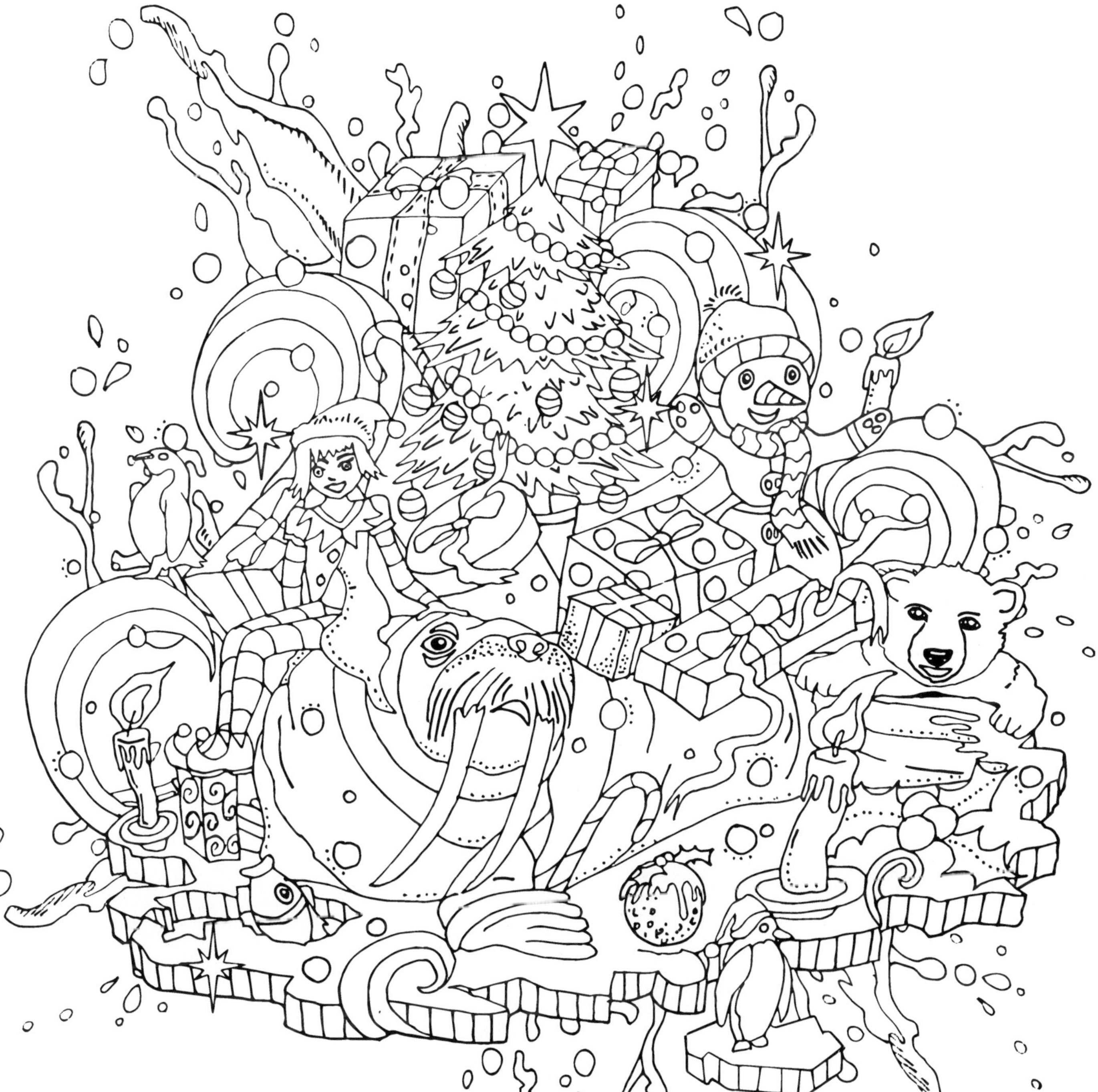

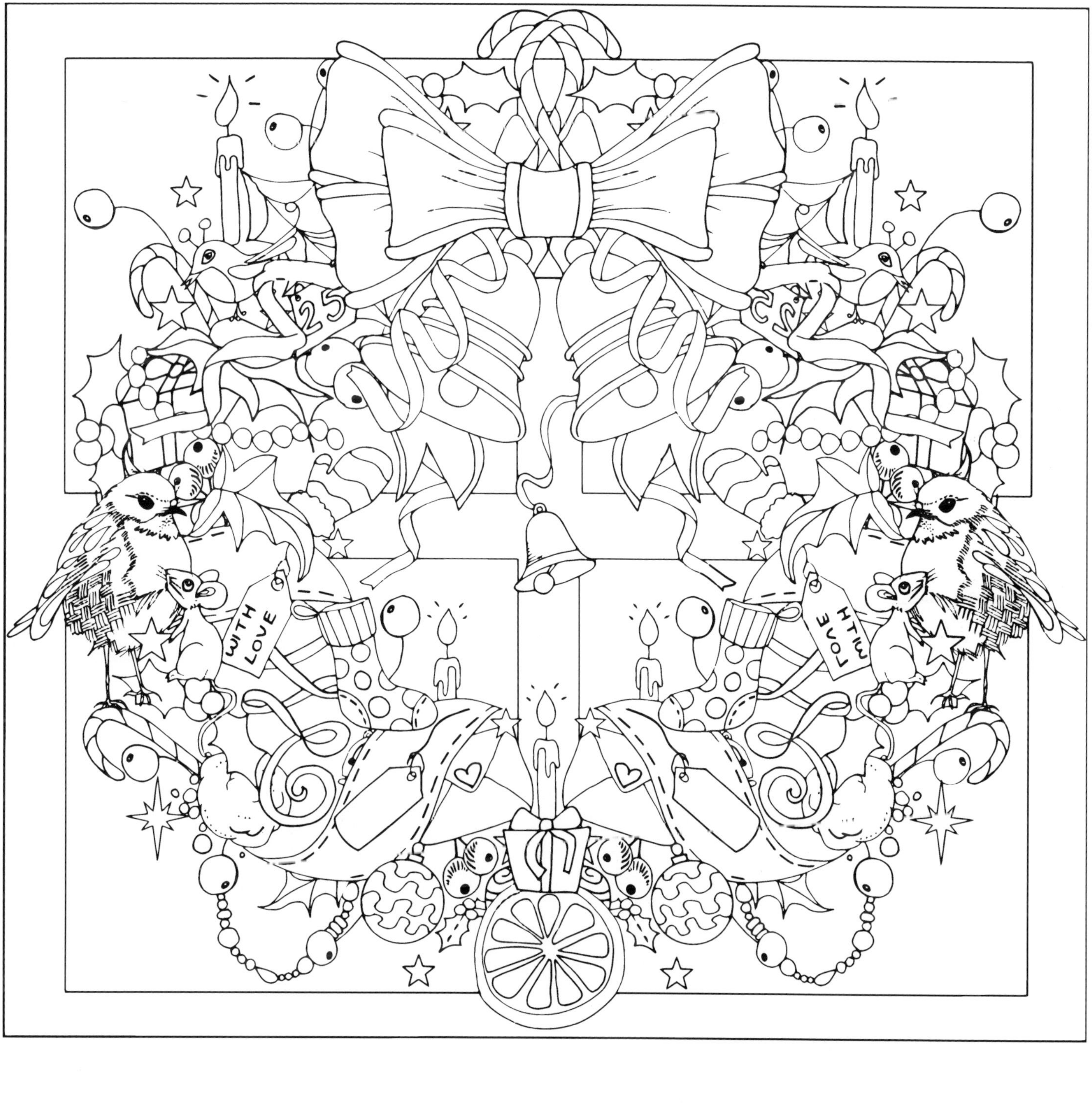
25
WITH LOVE

TEST PAGE

Test your colouring materials on this image

Printed in Poland
by Amazon Fulfillment
Poland Sp. z o.o., Wrocław